W9-CDH-026

HORSE SENSE

HORSE SENSE

There is just as much horse sense in the world as ever, but the horses have most of it.

Willow Creek Press

Published by Willow Creek Press
P.O. Box 147, Minocqua, Wisconsin 54548

Editor/Design: Andrea Donner

Library of Congress Cataloging-in-Publication Data
Horse sense : there is just as much horse sense as
ever, but the horses have most of it /
[editor/design, Andrea Donner].
p.cm.
ISBN 1-59543-057-1 (alk. paper)
1. Horses--Quotations, maxims, etc. 2. Horses--
Quotations, maxims, etc.--Translations into
English. I. Donner, Andrea K., 1967- II. Title.

PN6084.H66H65 2004
636.1--dc22

2004019809

Printed in Canada

opposite © Bob Langrish; left © Dusty L. Perin

The hooves of horses! Oh! Witching and sweet.
Is the music earth steals from the iron-shod feet;
No whisper of lover, no trilling bird,
Can stir me as much as hooves of horses have stirred.

Will H. Ogilvie

Courage, wisdom born of insight and humility, empathy born of compassion and love, all can be bequeathed by a horse to his rider.

Charles de Kunffy

An understanding of a horse's nature is one of the first basics in the art of riding, and all horsemen must make this their principle consideration.

Francois Robichon de la Gueriniere

The horse weighs one thousand pounds and I weigh ninety-five.
I guess I'd better get him to cooperate.

Jockey Steve Cauthen

Horses can educate through first hand, subjective, personal experiences, unlike human tutors, teachers and professors can ever do. Horses can build character, not merely urge one to improve on it. Horses forge the mind, the character, the emotions and inner lives of humans… In partnership with a horse, one is seldom lacking for thought, emotion and inspiration.

Charles de Kunffy

Knowledge is gained by learning; trust by doubt; skill by practice.

Thomas Szasz

There comes a time in life when there is nothing else to do but go your own way. Where you are headed there are no trails, no paths, just your own instincts.

Sergio Bambaren

Make voyages. Attempt them. There's nothing else.

Tennessee Williams

© M. Watson / Ardea.com

It is only by following your deepest instinct that you can lead a rich life.

Katharine Butler Hathaway

The larger the island of knowledge, the longer the shoreline of wonder.

Ralph W. Sockman

Not the senses I have but what I do with them is my kingdom.

Helen Keller

An unhurried sense of time is in itself a form of wealth.

Bonnie Friedman

*Slow down
and enjoy life.
It's not only the
scenery you
miss by going
too fast, you
also miss the
sense of where
you are going
and why.*

Eddie Cantor

Time, when it is left to itself and no definite demands are made on it, cannot be trusted to move at any recognized pace. Usually it loiters; but just when one has come to count upon its slowness, it may suddenly break into a wild irrational gallop.

Edith Wharton

Living in the moment brings you a sense of reverence for all of life's blessings.

Oprah Winfrey

To be satisfied with a little, is the greatest wisdom; and he that increaseth his riches, increaseth his cares; but a contented mind is a hidden treasure, and trouble findeth it not.

Akhenaton

Only in a quiet mind is adequate perception of the world.

Hans Margolius

Finish each day and be done with it. You have done what you could. Some blunders and absurdities no doubt crept in; forget them as soon as you can. Tomorrow is a new day; begin it well and serenely and with too high a spirit to be cumbered with your old nonsense.

Ralph Waldo Emerson

© Bob Langrish

The time you enjoy wasting is not wasted time.

Bertrand Russell

The art of being happy lies in the power of extracting happiness from common things.

Henry Ward Beecher

*Rest is not idleness, and
to lie sometimes on the
grass on a summer day
listening to the murmur of
water, or watching the
clouds float across the sky,
is hardly a waste of time.*

Sir J. Lubbock

*Consider this, the beauty and poetry
of a horse in motion, drawing its power
from the ground into the very air
through which it moves, like Pegasus reborn.*

Margot Page

opposite & left © Bob Langrish

Friend, our closeness is this: anywhere you put your foot,
feel me in the firmness under you.

Rumi

© Bob Langrish

Riding a horse is not a gentle hobby, to be picked up and laid down like a game of solitaire. It is a grand passion. It seizes a person whole and, once it has done so, he will have to accept that his life will be radically changed.

Ralph Waldo Emerson

Horse sense is the thing a horse has which keeps it from betting on people.

W.C. Fields

4

In a moment of decision, the best thing you can do is the right thing to do. The worst thing you can do is nothing.

Theodore Roosevelt

It is common sense to take a method and try it. If it fails, admit it frankly and try another. But above all, try something.

Franklin D. Roosevelt

Failure is, in a sense, the highway to success,
inasmuch as every discovery of what is false leads us
to seek earnestly after what is true, and every
fresh experience points out some form of error
which we shall afterwards carefully avoid.

John Keats

We become brave by performing brave actions. Aristotle

One is happy as a result of one's own efforts.

George Sand

The highest of distinctions is service to others.

King George VI

Everyone enjoys doing the kind of work for which he is best suited.

Napoleon Hill

Life is much less a competitive struggle for survival than a triumph of cooperation and creativity.

Fritjof Capra

Monotony is the law of nature. Look at the monotonous manner in which the sun rises. The monotony of necessary occupations is exhilarating and life-giving.

Gandhi

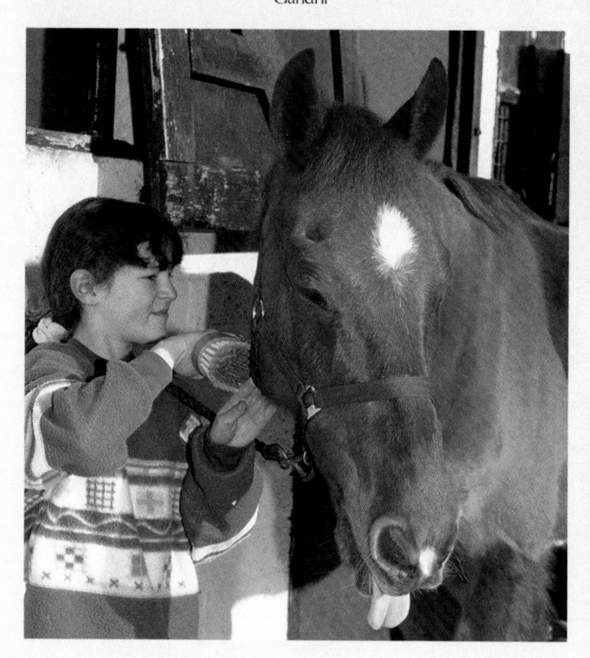

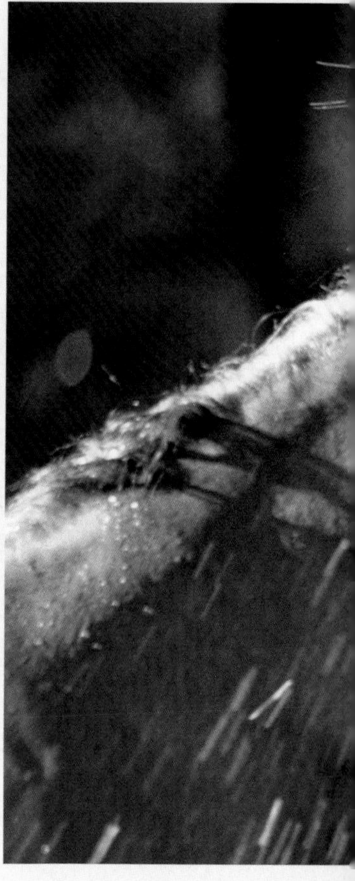

The strength of a man's virtue should not be measured by his special exertions, but by his habitual acts.

Blaise Pascal

There is no enlightenment outside of daily life.

Thich Nhat Hanh

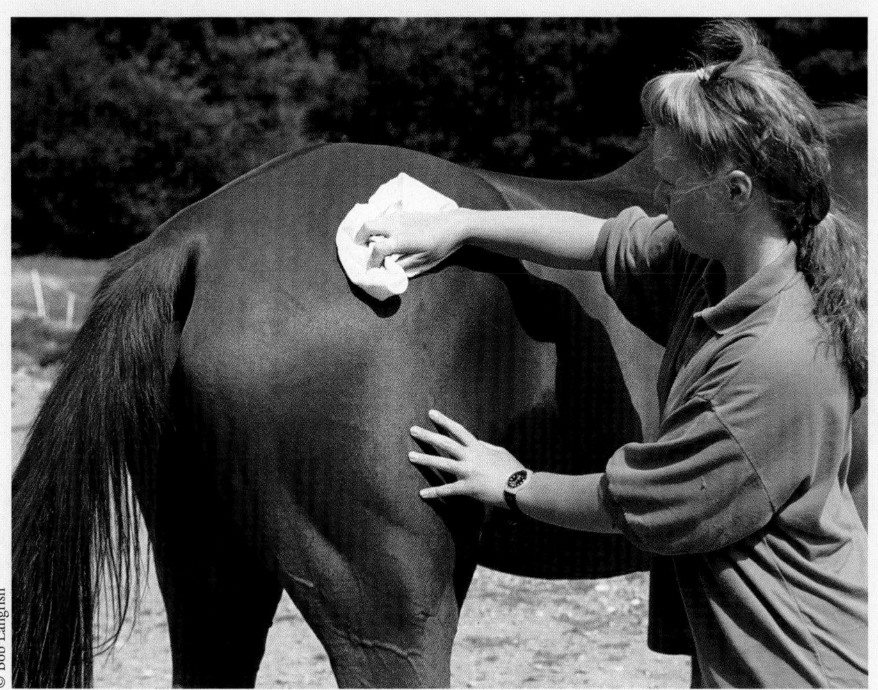

We are of the earth,
made of the same stuff;
there is no other, no division
between us and the "lower"
or "higher" forms of being.

Estella Lauder

© Lynn M. Stone

Whatever peace I know rests in the natural world,
in feeling myself a part of it, even in a small way.

May Sarton

Do not wish to be anything but what you are, and try to be that perfectly.

St. Francis de Sales

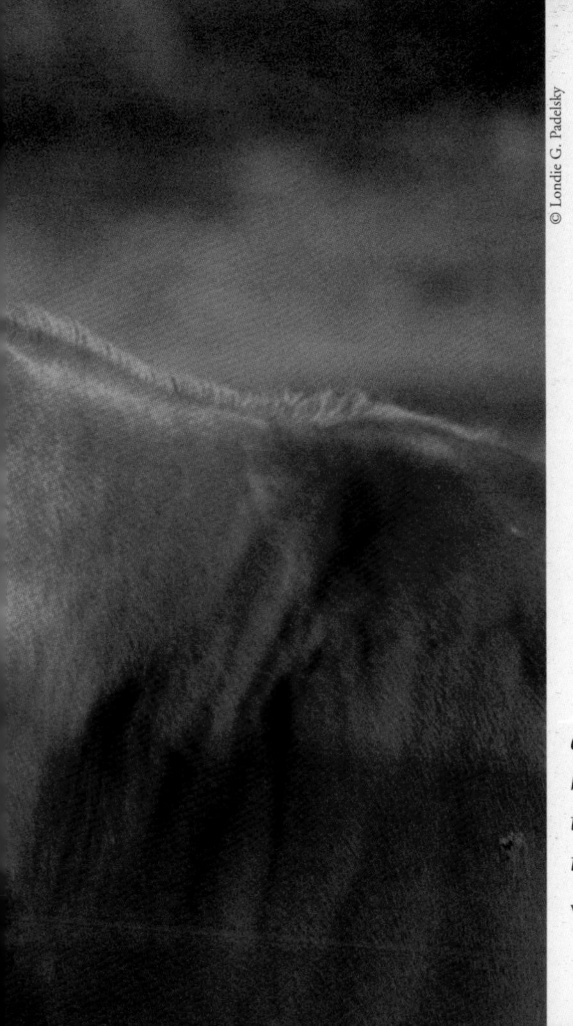

It is hard for the face to conceal the thoughts of the heart — the true character of the soul. — The look without is an index of what is within.

William Shakespeare

Our happiness in this world depends on the affections we are able to inspire.

Duchess Prazlin

opposite & left © Bob Langrish

We are shaped and fashioned by what we love.

Johann Wolfgang von Goethe

*So much of what
is best in us in
bound up in our love
of family, that it
remains the measure
of our stability because
it measures our sense
of loyalty. All other
pacts of love or fear
derive from it and are
modeled upon it.*

Haniel Long

left & opposite © Bob Langrish

A friend may
well be reckoned
the masterpiece
of nature.

Ralph Waldo Emerson

A faithful friend is the medicine of life.

Ecclesiasticus 6:16

Our perfect companions
never have fewer than four feet.

Colette

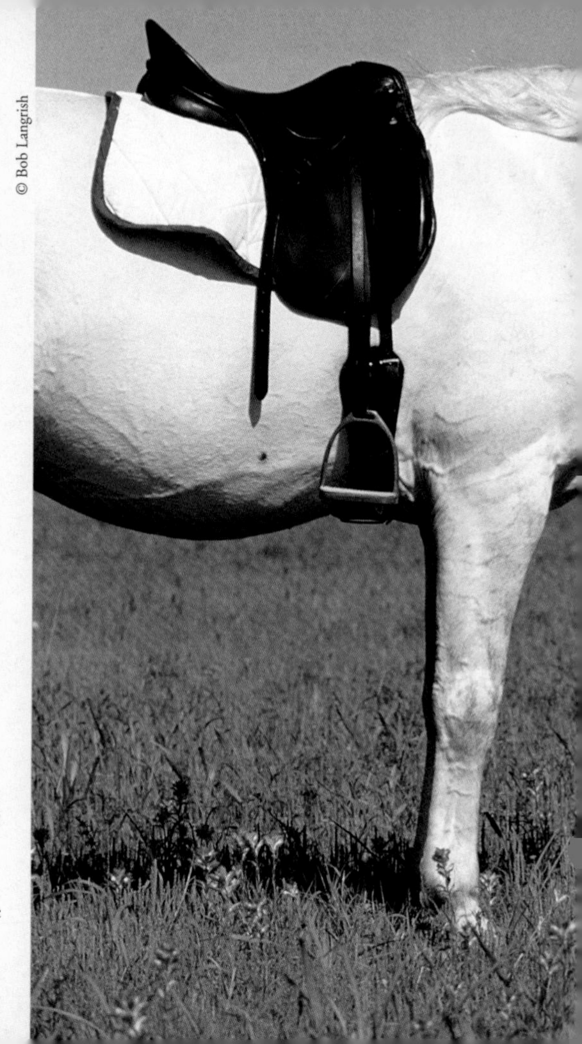

© Bob Langrish

It takes two to speak the truth —
one to speak, and another to hear.

Henry David Thoreau

© Bob Langrish

'Tis the privilege of friendship to talk nonsense,
and have nonsense respected.

Charles Lamb

Talk sense to a fool and he calls you foolish.

Euripides

Advice is one of those things it is far more blessed to give than to receive.

Carolyn Wells

© Bob Langrish

© Bob Langrish

Accept good advice gracefully — as long as it doesn't interfere with what you intended to do in the first place.

Gene Brown

He deserves paradise who makes his companions laugh.

The Koran

© Bob Langrish

The old believe everything; the middle-aged suspect everything; the young know everything.

Oscar Wilde

Play is the beginning of knowledge.

George Dorsey

opposite & left © Bob Langrish

If I were to wish for anything, I should not wish for wealth and power, but for the passionate sense of potential — for the eye which, ever young and ardent, sees the possible. Pleasure disappoints; possibility never.

Soren Kierkegaard

God forbid that I should go to any heaven in which there are no horses.

R. Graham

Horses change lives. They give our young people confidence and self-esteem. They provide peace and tranquility to troubled souls — they give us hope!

Toni Robinson